great
tapas

D0764494

great tapas

THE ESSENCE OF SPAIN IN DELICIOUSLY
AUTHENTIC SNACKS AND APPETIZERS

SILVANA FRANCO

LORENZ BOOKS

This edition published by Lorenz Books

© Anness Publishing Limited 1996, 1999

LORENZ BOOKS are available for bulk purchase for sales promotion
and for premium use. For details, write or call the sales director,
Lorenz Books, 27 West 20th Street, New York, NY 10011;
(800) 354-9657

Lorenz Books is an imprint of Anness Publishing Inc.

All rights reserved. No part of this publication may be reproduced,
stored in a retrieval system, or transmitted in any way or by any means,
electronic, mechanical, photocopying, recording or otherwise, without
the prior written permission of the copyright holder.

ISBN 0-7548-0266-3

Publisher: Joanna Lorenz
Senior Cookery Editor: Linda Fraser
Designer: Siân Keogh
Photography and styling: Patrick McLeavey
Food for photography: Jacqueline Clark
Illustrator: Madeleine David

Front Cover: Sam Stowell, Photographer; Helen Trent, Stylist;
Angela Boggiano, Home Economist

Printed and bound in Hong Kong/China

1 3 5 7 9 10 8 6 4 2

NOTE
Medium eggs should be used unless otherwise stated.

PICTURE CREDITS
*Picture on pages 2–3: Janet Bligh, The Anthony Blake Photo Library;
page 6: The Anthony Blake Photo Library; and page 7: Brian Seed,
Aspect Picture Library.*

CONTENTS

INTRODUCTION

Tapas originated in Andalucia where the long summer days and warm summer evenings merge into one, and the people of southern Spain who gather outdoors on pavements and verandas enjoy lively conversation, a glass of chilled, golden fino sherry and a tasty snack typical of the region. The tradition of serving tapas with drinks is a custom that has spread from Spain to all the major cities of Europe and beyond. The word "tapa" actually means "lid", for in the past every glass of sherry bought in a local Spanish bar would come covered by a slice of bread topped with ham, cheese or fried black pudding to keep out the flies. Sadly, finding complimentary tapas is pretty rare these days, but instead we have vibrant bars offering a vast selection.

Mealtimes in Spain are lengthy affairs with a sizeable lunch served around two o'clock and dinner eaten at about ten in the evening. So, when hunger strikes in that long gap between meals, Spaniards head for their local tapas bar for something quick to eat and to catch up on the local gossip.

Tapas bars offer a fantastic variety of dishes, which make good use of colorful, flavorsome, home-produced ingredients such as extra virgin olive oil and vine-ripened tomatoes. Many bars offer house specialties featuring ingredients indigenous to the particular area, such as homemade blood sausage dishes or locally caught sardines. Whatever is on offer, the surroundings are guaranteed to be informal, friendly and more often than not, pretty lively.

Since the days when tapas was served as edible covers for glasses of sherry, the range of these delectable snacks has increased tremendously, but they are still ultimately designed for easy eating, so that their consumption disrupts the conversation as little as possible. Because of this, few tapas require cutlery and many of the morsels come on chunks of bread or speared with toothpicks. There are, of course, exceptions to the rule. If you plan to tackle tapas, be prepared to get your fingers dirty. Shelling shrimp that are swimming in a pungent garlic oil is no job for the fastidious, but the rewards are marvelous, so standing on ceremony is *de rigueur* for the dedicated tapas eater. In fact, some of the older tapas bars positively encourage the tossing aside of shellfish peelings by providing a carpet of fresh sawdust on the floor.

Although the tapas themselves are no longer included in the price of a sherry, the selection that's available in modern bars is usually quite amazing. There may be as many as fifty different types on offer, many of them displayed on the bar

Traditional tapas depend on the use of the best home-produced ingredients: chorizo, anchovies, olives and farmhouse cheese.

counter with an eye to color. A plate of fried potatoes may have as its partner bright red pimientos, and the choice may include anything from simple fried almonds or chunks of cured sausage to a sophisticated dish of stuffed mussels.

This comprehensive collection of recipes has been put together with the home-cook in mind. The dishes are all very simple to make and none requires any specialized equipment. Many of the traditional tapas, such as *tortilla* and *patatas bravas,* are included, as well as plenty of contemporary dishes made from classic Spanish ingredients such as chorizo and pimientos. These modern dishes can very happily be served in conjunction with the traditional tapas to provide a balanced selection. Many of the tapas are based on bread or vegetables, so there is also a good choice for vegetarians. Lots of the tapas are served cold and are great for easy picnicking or barbecuing.

There are no hard and fast rules when it comes to eating and serving tapas, although portions do tend to be small and varied. Nor are there any schedules to adhere to; unlike formal meals, tapas can be enjoyed at any time of the day.

Most tapas dishes are quick and easy to prepare, and some of the best, such as stuffed olives, salted nuts, cubes of cheese and pickled capers, are virtually instant – ideal for serving as impromptu nibbles.

When serving tapas remember that, traditionally, they are not intended to be eaten as a main course meal, but rather as a small snack and accompaniment to a glass of sherry. If you do plan to serve tapas as a meal, mix and match a selection of dishes – choose one or two simple fish, meat or vegetable dishes and pair with something with sauce, or serve a crisp, fried dish to give a wealth of flavor, texture and color. For a main meal, offer at least six different tapas to satisfy your guests' appetites.

Tapas are the perfect accompaniment to lively conversation and warm companionship. With these recipes in your repertoire, entertaining will always be a pleasure.

Friendly surroundings and a lively atmosphere typify the traditional tapas bar, where a vast array of delicious tapas are on offer.

GLOSSARY OF SPANISH FOODS

Aceite – oil
Aceituna – olive
Ajo – garlic
Albóndiga – meatball
Alioli or *Aïoli* – garlic mayonnaise from Catalonia
Almandras – almonds
Almejas – clams
Anchoa or *Boquerón* – anchovy
Arroz – rice
Azafran – saffron
Bacalao – salt cod
Chipirones or *chopitos* – small squid
Chorizo – pork and paprika sausage, usually cured
Gambas – shrimp
Hígado – liver

Huevo – egg
Jamón – ham
Jerez – sherry
Manchego – ewe milk cheese
Morcilla – black pudding from Asturias
Pan – bread
Patatas – potatoes
Perejil – parsley
Pescado – fish
Pollo – chicken
Queso – cheese
Salsa – sauce
Sidra – cider
Tascas – tapas bars
Tortilla – omelet
Vieiras – scallops

INGREDIENTS

BLACK PUDDING

This is an important ingredient all over Spain. Different regions have their own specialized "blood sausage" but probably the most common is *morcilla*. This is flavored with garlic, marjoram and paprika and various other ingredients, such as cilantro, chili and red wine.

CHEESE

Manchego, made from ewe milk, originates from La Mancha and is available in various stages of maturation. It is very difficult to find a soft and creamy young Manchego outside Spain; however, it is quite widely available from cheese shops and continental delis as a tangy, full-flavored, hard cheese.

Monte Enebro is a delicious soft goat cheese. It has a good, strong flavor without being overpowering.

Picos Blue, which comes from the Cabrales region in northern Spain, is wrapped in maple leaves.

CHORIZO

Chorizo is a pork sausage flavored with paprika. It is readily available in a selection of shapes and sizes in both smoked and unsmoked varieties. Although it is generally sold cured and ready-to-eat, it is possible to find fresh chorizo that needs to be cooked before eating. All the recipes in this book call for the cured variety.

Clockwise from bottom left: sliced chorizo, jamón serrano, chorizo sausages and black pudding.

Full-flavored Spanish cheeses for cooking or eating, from left: Picos Blue, Manchego and Monte Enebro.

CLAMS

Clams come in a wide range of different sizes and varieties. Small ones – a little larger than cockles, similar to the type used in the classic Italian dish *Spaghetti Vongole* – are recommended for the recipes in this book, but you can use any type and adjust the cooking times accordingly. Prepare and cook as for mussels (see below).

GARLIC

Garlic is a very popular flavoring ingredient in Spanish cooking and features prominently in a number of tapas. The amount you use is largely a matter of personal taste. There are white-skinned, pink-skinned and purple-skinned varieties – the latter is generally considered to be the best.

JAMON SERRANO

This delicious salt-cured ham is rosy pink in color and is eaten raw. It is sold on deli counters, carved into paper-thin slices. Other cured hams which can be used instead include Italian Parma ham, or prosciutto, and Belgian Jambon d'Ardennes.

MUSSELS

Whenever possible, choose fresh, live mussels. Soak them in cold water for about 1 hour before cooking and always use on the day of purchase. Scrape off any barnacles with a round-bladed knife, then pull out any gritty beards still attached to the mussels. Before cooking, sharply tap any open mussels with a knife and discard any that don't close immediately. To simply steam the mussels, place them in a large, covered pan with a splash of wine or water, cover and cook for about 2–5 minutes, depending upon the size, until all the shells have opened. Mussels are naturally salty, so do not add any extra. Discard any mussels that remain closed.

It is often said that mussels should never be cooked twice, and it is true that there is nothing worse than an over-cooked, soggy mussel that is starting to disintegrate, but provided they are not initially over-done, they can happily be added to other dishes such as *paella* or briefly cooked again, as in the mouthwatering Broiled Mussels with Parsley and Parmesan on page 34.

OLIVES

All the olives we see in stores have been cured, as they are not edible straight from the tree. Where possible, choose olives with their pits in and pit them yourself. It is preferable to buy them loose in brine rather than packed in oil; keep them in the fridge and use within a few days.

PAPRIKA

This is a very popular seasoning made from ground red bell pepper. It is very mild and can be used generously to add flavor and vibrant color to many Spanish dishes.

ROASTED BELL PEPPERS

Roasted bell peppers are more often cooked under the broiler than actually roasted in an oven. Although it is quicker to halve the peppers before broiling them, it is much better to keep them whole so that any juice released during cooking is contained inside the peppers. Place the peppers on a wire rack or broiler tray and place under a hot broiler for 10–12 minutes, turning them occasionally, until the skins have blistered and blackened. Remove from the heat and cover with a clean dish towel; let stand for a few minutes so the steam helps to soften the skin and lift it away from the flesh. Holding the pepper in the dish towel, make a small hole in the bottom and gently squeeze the juices into a small bowl. Peel away the papery skin, then halve the pepper and remove the core and seeds.

SAFFRON

The most expensive spice in the world, saffron consists of the dark orange stigmas from flowering crocuses. The best saffron comes from La Mancha in Spain, although other countries do produce it. It has a fairly short shelf-life and should be infused in a little liquid such as wine or water before being used. Saffron is the key flavoring in the Spanish national dish, *paella*. It should be used sparingly as too much will give an unpleasant, almost soapy flavor.

SALT COD

Salt cod comes in two basic types: fully dried and semi-dried. *Bacalao*, the Spanish salt cod, usually displayed as a whole fish, is fully dried. It needs a good 48 hours soaking in cold water to remove the salt and plump up the flesh, by which time it will be at least three times its original size. It is important to change the water every few hours.

Aromatic flavoring ingredients for tapas include (clockwise from the top): fresh garlic, paprika and saffron threads.

Clockwise from bottom left: fresh mussels, clams, squid and salt cod.

The second type of salt cod is semi-dried and can be found, in packages containing smaller pieces, in ethnic stores. As it is less dry, it only needs about 24 hours soaking and does not swell as much. It can be used in place of *bacalao*, if necessary.

SCALLOPS

Most fishmongers sell scallops in their shells. Like clams, there are a number of different types and sizes, including the little queens (ideal for broiling with brown butter, see page 36).

To open a scallop, place it on a level surface with the flat shell uppermost. Slide a thin-bladed knife between the shells and cut the muscle which keeps the scallop closed. Lift off the top shell and pull out the gray frill around the scallop flesh. Carefully cut the meat out of the bottom shell, keeping the plump orange coral intact.

To cook the scallop, sear it briefly on a hot, oiled griddle or heavy-bottomed frying pan; if you intend returning it to the half-shell to serve, first rinse and dry the shell out thoroughly.

SHERRY

Sherry is a very valuable cooking ingredient – dry sherry can be used in place of white wine in any of the recipes here. It should be kept chilled and used soon after opening. Sweet sherries add a lovely flavor to many savory dishes and are particularly good with meat dishes such as Chicken Livers in Sherry, see page 68.

SQUID

Squid can be bought pre-cleaned and even cut into rings, but to prepare it yourself, gently pull the tentacles with the intestines attached away from the body. You may spot the ink sac with the intestines, this can be kept if desired, but the remainder should be discarded. Cut the edible tentacles off the head just above the eyes and remove, then pull out and discard the tough central beak. Peel the thin purple skin away from the white body and pull off the two fins. Thoroughly rinse the body tube, fins and tentacles.

COLD TAPAS

Cold tapas are a staple in most bars. Tasty snacks such as crunchy bread sticks, fried almonds or stuffed olives are often to be found lining the bar or tables in busy tascas. There is a wonderful selection of dishes in this chapter – choose from classic Marinated Olives, Sweet and Salty Beet Chips, or melt-in-the-mouth Olive and Anchovy Bites. Many of the dishes can be made ahead of time, ready to be presented to unexpected guests, and are also good for packing into lunch boxes and picnic baskets.

Marinated Olives

For the best flavor, marinate the olives for at least 10 days and serve at room temperature.

INGREDIENTS

Serves 4

1⅓ cups unpitted, green olives
3 garlic cloves
1 teaspoon coriander seeds
2 small red chilies
2 – 3 thick slices of lemon, cut into pieces
1 thyme or rosemary sprig
5 tablespoons white wine vinegar

─── COOK'S TIP ───

For a change, use a mix of caraway and cumin seeds in place of the coriander.

1 Spread out the olives and garlic on a chopping board. Using a rolling pin, crack and flatten them slightly.

2 Crack the coriander seeds in a mortar with a pestle.

3 Mix the olives, garlic, coriander seeds, chilies, lemon pieces, herb sprig and wine vinegar in a large bowl. Toss well, then transfer the mixture to a clean glass jar. Pour in water to cover. Store in the fridge for at least 5 days before serving.

Salted Almonds

These crunchy salted nuts are at their best when fresh, so, if you can, cook them on the day you plan to eat them.

INGREDIENTS

Serves 2 – 4

1 cup whole almonds in their skins
1 tablespoon egg white, lightly beaten
½ teaspoon coarse sea salt

─── COOK'S TIP ───

This traditional method of salt-roasting nuts gives a matte, dry-looking finish; if you want them to shine, turn the roasted nuts into a bowl, add 1 tablespoon of olive oil and shake well to mix.

1 Preheat the oven to 350°F. Spread out the almonds on a baking sheet and roast for about 20 minutes, until cracked and golden.

2 Mix the egg white and salt in a bowl, add the almonds and shake well to coat.

3 Turn out onto the baking sheet, give a shake to separate the nuts, then return them to the oven for 5 minutes, until they have dried. Let rest until cold, then store in an airtight container until ready to serve.

Eggplant Paste

Serve this velvet-textured dip in the summertime, when there is a ready supply of firm, glossy eggplant and crisp vegetables to serve it with.

INGREDIENTS

Serves 4

1 large eggplant
2 tablespoons olive oil
2 garlic cloves, finely chopped
2 tablespoons chopped fresh cilantro
juice of ½ lemon
½ teaspoon cayenne pepper
salt and freshly ground black pepper
fresh cilantro, to garnish

1 Preheat the oven to 400°F. Place the eggplant on a baking sheet and cook for 30 minutes, until the skin is blackened and the eggplant is very soft.

2 Let the eggplant cool slightly. Cut it in half and use a tablespoon to scoop out the flesh into a bowl; discard the skin.

3 Mash the eggplant flesh using a fork to form a paste.

4 Stir in the olive oil, garlic, cilantro and lemon juice, with enough cayenne, salt and pepper to suit your taste. Let cool and then serve garnished with cilantro.

─ COOK'S TIP ─

If preferred, the eggplant can be broiled for 20 minutes; turn it frequently.

Marinated Pimientos

Pimientos are simply cooked, skinned bell peppers. You can buy them in cans or jars, but they are much tastier if homemade.

INGREDIENTS

Serves 2–4
3 red bell peppers
2 small garlic cloves, crushed
3 tablespoons chopped fresh parsley
1 tablespoon sherry vinegar
2 tablespoons olive oil
salt

1 Preheat the broiler to high. Place the bell peppers on a baking sheet and broil for 8–12 minutes, turning occasionally, until the skins have blistered and blackened. Remove from the heat, cover with a clean dish towel and let stand for 5 minutes, so that the steam softens the skin.

2 Make a small cut in the bottom of each pepper and squeeze out the juice into a pitcher. Peel away the skin and cut both peppers in half. Remove and discard the core and seeds.

3 Using a sharp knife, cut each pepper in half lengthwise into ½-inch wide strips. Place them in a small bowl.

4 Whisk the garlic, parsley, vinegar and oil into the pepper juices. Add salt to taste. Pour over the pepper strips and toss well. Cover and chill, but, if possible, bring the bell peppers back to room temperature before serving.

Chick-pea Paste

INGREDIENTS

Serves 4

14-ounce can chick-peas, drained
2 small garlic cloves, halved
4 tablespoons parsley leaves
4 tablespoons olive oil
2 tablespoons freshly squeezed
  lemon juice
salt and freshly ground black pepper
fresh parsley, to garnish

— COOK'S TIP —

For a change, try making this tapas dish with other canned beans such as cannellini beans or kidney beans.

1 Blend the chick-peas, garlic and herbs in a food processor or blender until finely chopped. With the motor running, slowly pour in the olive oil and lemon juice to make a thick paste.

2 Add salt and pepper to taste. Spoon into a bowl, cover the paste and chill until ready to serve, garnished with a sprig of parsley.

Sweet and Salty Beet Chips

For a real treat, serve these brightly colored chips with a bowl of freshly made aïoli – the delicious garlicky mayonnaise.

INGREDIENTS

Serves 2

1 small fresh beet
superfine sugar
fine salt and coarse sea salt
vegetable oil, for frying

1 Peel the beet and slice it very thinly, using a mandolin or a swivel-style vegetable peeler.

2 Lay the slices out on paper towels and sprinkle them lightly with sugar and salt.

— COOK'S TIP —

Beet chips are especially flavorsome, but other naturally sweet vegetables, such as carrot and sweet potato, also taste delicious when cooked like this. Make several different varieties, if you like, and serve them on a large, flat platter or heaped in separate small bowls – they make ideal party nibbles.

---

3 Pour oil to a depth of 2 inches into a deep saucepan, then heat until a cube of bread turns golden in less than 1 minute. Cook the beet slices in batches for 1–2 minutes, until they float to the surface and turn golden brown around the edges. Drain on paper towels and let cool.

Pork Cracklings

These crisp savory bites can be made well ahead, if you like. Store them in an airtight container for up to 2 weeks before serving.

INGREDIENTS

Serves 4
4 ounces pork rind
vegetable oil, for frying
paprika
sea salt

COOK'S TIP

Although paprika can vary from fairly mild to hot, it isn't fiery hot – if you'd like to make these a little spicier, add a pinch of chili powder to the paprika.

1 Using a sharp knife, cut the pork rind into strips about ½ inch wide and 1 inch long.

2 Pour vegetable oil to a depth of 1 inch into a deep, heavy-bottomed frying pan. Heat the oil until a cube of bread browns in 1 minute. Cook the strips of rind in the oil for 1–2 minutes, until puffed up and golden. Drain on paper towels and sprinkle with paprika and salt to taste. Serve hot or cold.

Banderillas

These miniature skewers are very popular in the tapas bars of northern Spain. They are generally made from a variety of pickled vegetables, but often also include cured or pickled fish, hard-boiled eggs, cooked shrimp, tuna and cured meats. Make sure that you eat this simple but classic *banderilla* in a single mouthful!

INGREDIENTS

Serves 4
12 small capers
12 drained anchovy fillets in oil
12 pitted black olives
12 cornichons or small gherkins
12 silverskin pickled onions

1 Place a caper at one end of each anchovy fillet and roll up.

2 Thread 1 caper-filled anchovy, 1 olive, 1 cornichon or gherkin and 1 pickled onion onto each of 12 toothpicks. Chill and serve.

COOK'S TIP

For a truly authentic *banderilla*, wrap a little square of colored paper around the tip of the toothpick, so they resemble the bull-fighting dart that they are named after.

Marinated Anchovies

Make these at least 1 hour and up to 24 hours in advance. Fresh anchovies are tiny, so be prepared to spend time filleting them – the results will be worth the effort.

Ingredients

Serves 4

8 ounces fresh anchovies
juice of 3 lemons
2 tablespoons extra virgin olive oil
2 garlic cloves, finely chopped
1 tablespoon chopped fresh parsley
flaked sea salt

1 Cut off the ends from the anchovies, then split them open down one side.

2 Open each anchovy out flat and carefully lift out the bone.

3 Arrange the anchovies skin-side down in a single layer on a plate. Pour over two-thirds of the lemon juice and sprinkle with the salt. Cover and let stand for 1–24 hours, basting occasionally with the juices, until the flesh is white and no longer translucent.

4 Transfer the fish to a serving plate and drizzle over the olive oil and the remaining lemon juice. Sprinkle the garlic and parsley over the top, cover and chill until ready to serve.

Olive and Anchovy Bites

These melt-in-the-mouth morsels store very well; freeze them for up to 3 months, or keep in an airtight container for up to 2 weeks before serving.

INGREDIENTS

Makes 40 – 45

1 cup all-purpose flour
½ cup chilled butter
1 cup finely grated cheese, such as
 Manchego, aged Cheddar
  or Gruyère
2-ounce can anchovy fillets in oil,
 drained and coarsely chopped
⅓ cup pitted, black olives,
 coarsely chopped
½ teaspoon cayenne pepper
sea salt

COOK'S TIP

For a change, sprinkle the olive and anchovy bites with finely grated Parmesan cheese, or dust lightly with cayenne pepper before baking.

1 Place the flour, butter, cheese, anchovies, olives and cayenne in a food processor or blender and pulse until the mixture forms a firm dough.

2 Wrap the dough loosely in plastic wrap. Chill for 20 minutes.

3 Preheat the oven to 400°F. Roll out the dough thinly on a lightly floured surface.

4 Cut the dough into 2-inch wide strips, then cut across each strip diagonally, in alternate directions, to make small triangles. Transfer the triangles to baking sheets and bake for 8 – 10 minutes until golden. Cool on a wire rack. Sprinkle with sea salt before serving.

Sesame Bread Sticks

Bread sticks are one of the most versatile of tapas dishes. Try serving them with *Banderillas* and a bowl of aïoli, or simply accompanied by a glass of red wine for dipping them into.

INGREDIENTS

Makes 30
2 cups white bread flour
1 teaspoon salt
¼ ounce fast-rising dried yeast
2 tablespoons sesame seeds
2 tablespoons olive oil

COOK'S TIP

Bread sticks can be made with many different flavorings – try using fennel seeds, poppy seeds or finely grated Parmesan cheese instead of sesame seeds. They are best eaten fresh, so don't make them more than a day or two in advance. Store them in an airtight container until ready to eat.

1 Preheat the oven to 450°F. Sift the flour into a bowl. Stir in the salt, yeast and sesame seeds and make a well in the center.

2 Add the olive oil to the flour mixture and enough warm water to make a firm dough. Turn out the dough onto a lightly floured surface and knead for 5–10 minutes until smooth and elastic.

3 Rub a little oil onto the surface of the dough. Return it to the clean bowl and cover with a clean dish towel. Let the dough rise in a warm place for about 40 minutes, or until it has doubled in size.

4 Punch down the dough, then knead lightly until smooth. Pull off small balls of dough, then, using your hands, roll out each ball on a lightly floured surface to a thin sausage about 10 inches long.

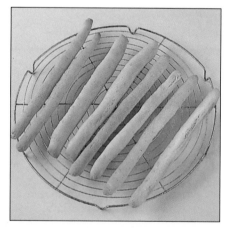

5 Place the bread sticks on baking sheets and bake for 15 minutes, until crisp and golden. Cool the bread sticks on a wire rack, then store them in an airtight container until needed.

SEAFOOD TAPAS

Seafood plays a major role in Spanish cooking. Clams, scallops, mussels and the little chipirones (baby squid) make ideal, bite-size tapas. Although the preparation of some seafood may be lengthy, it can all be done well ahead, and the actual cooking time is usually very short. In order to bring out the delicate flavor of the seafood, many of these tapas have been very simply prepared – pan-fried, broiled or steamed with little more than butter, garlic and a handful of fresh herbs, although there are the odd fancier exceptions such as the delicious Butterflied Shrimp in Chocolate Sauce.

Jumbo Shrimp in Sherry

INGREDIENTS

Serves 4

12 raw jumbo shrimp, shelled
2 tablespoons olive oil
2 tablespoons sherry
few drops of Tabasco sauce
salt and freshly ground black pepper

1 Make a shallow cut down the back of each shrimp, then pull out and discard the dark intestinal tract.

2 Heat the oil in a frying pan and fry the shrimp for 2–3 minutes until pink. Pour over the sherry and season with Tabasco sauce, salt and pepper. Turn into a dish and serve immediately.

Sizzling Shrimp

This dish works especially well with tiny shrimp that can be eaten whole, but any type of shrimp in the shell will be fine. Choose a small casserole or frying pan that can be taken to the table for serving while the shrimp are still sizzling.

INGREDIENTS

Serves 4

2 garlic cloves, halved
2 tablespoons butter
1 small red chili, seeded and
   finely sliced
4 ounces cooked shrimp, in the shell
sea salt and coarsely ground
   black pepper
lime wedges, to serve

1 Rub the cut surfaces of the garlic cloves over the surface of a frying pan, then throw them away. Add the butter to the pan and melt over fairly high heat until it just begins to turn golden brown.

2 Toss in the chili and shrimp. Stir-fry for 1–2 minutes until heated through, then season to taste and serve with lime wedges to squeeze over.

COOK'S TIP

Wear gloves when handling chilies, or wash your hands thoroughly afterwards, as the juices can cause severe irritation to sensitive skin, especially around the eyes, nose or mouth.

Butterflied Shrimp in Chocolate Sauce

Although the combination of flavors may seem odd, this is a truly delicious tapas. The use of bitter chocolate as a flavoring in savory dishes is popular.

INGREDIENTS

Serves 4

8 large raw shrimp, in the shell
1 tablespoon seasoned flour
1 tablespoon dry sherry
juice of 4 clementines or 1 large orange
½ ounce unsweetened, dark chocolate, chopped
2 tablespoons olive oil
2 garlic cloves, finely chopped
1-inch piece fresh ginger, finely chopped
1 small red chili, seeded and chopped
salt and freshly ground black pepper

1 Peel the shrimp, leaving just the tail sections intact. Make a shallow cut down the back of each shrimp and carefully pull out and discard the dark intestinal tract. Turn over the shrimp so that the undersides are uppermost, then carefully split them open from tail to top, using a small, sharp knife, cutting almost, but not quite, to the back.

2 Press the shrimp down firmly to flatten them out. Coat with the seasoned flour and set aside.

3 Gently heat the sherry and clementine or orange juice in a small saucepan. When warm, remove from the heat and stir in the chopped chocolate until melted.

4 Heat the olive oil in a frying pan. Fry the garlic, ginger and chili over medium heat for 2 minutes until golden. Remove with a slotted spoon and reserve. Add the shrimp, cut side down, to the pan and cook for 2–3 minutes until golden brown with pink edges. Turn and cook for 2 minutes more.

5 Return the garlic mixture to the pan and pour over the chocolate sauce. Cook for 1 minute, turning the shrimp to coat them in the glossy sauce. Season to taste and serve hot.

Jumbo Shrimp in Crispy Batter

Serve with an oriental-style dipping sauce, or offer a simple tomato sauce or lemon wedges.

INGREDIENTS

Serves 4

½ cup water
1 egg
1 cup all-purpose flour
1 teaspoon cayenne pepper
12 raw jumbo shrimp, in the shell
vegetable oil, for deep frying
lemon wedge and Italian parsley,
    to garnish

For the dipping sauce

2 tablespoons soy sauce
2 tablespoons dry sherry
2 teaspoons honey

1 In a large bowl, whisk the water with the egg. Add the flour and cayenne, and whisk until smooth.

2 Carefully shell the shrimp, leaving just the tail sections intact. Make a shallow cut down the back of each shrimp, then pull out and discard the dark intestinal tract.

3 To make the dipping sauce, stir together the soy sauce, dry sherry and honey in a small bowl.

4 Heat the oil in a large saucepan or deep-fryer, until a cube of bread browns in 1 minute.

5 Holding the shrimp by their tails, dip them into the batter, one at a time, shaking off any excess. Drop the shrimp carefully into the oil and fry for 2–3 minutes until crisp and golden brown. Drain on paper towels and serve with the dipping sauce, garnished with a lemon wedge and parsley.

COOK'S TIP

If you have any batter left over, use it to coat thin strips of vegetable such as sweet potato, beet, carrot or bell pepper, or use small broccoli florets or whole baby spinach leaves. Deep-fry until golden.

Seafood Salad

INGREDIENTS

Serves 6

4 ounces prepared squid rings
1 large carrot
6 crisp lettuce leaves, torn into pieces
4-inch piece cucumber, finely diced
12 fresh mussels, in their
  shells, steamed
4 ounces cooked, shelled shrimp
1 tablespoon drained capers

For the dressing
2 tablespoons freshly squeezed
  lemon juice
3 tablespoons olive oil
1 tablespoon chopped fresh parsley
sea salt and freshly ground black pepper

> ——— COOK'S TIP ———
>
> For a change, use any type of cooked
> seafood or fish in this salad – try steamed
> clams or cockles, shrimp in their shells or
> cubes of firm fish.

1 Place the squid rings in a metal strainer or vegetable steamer. Place over a saucepan of simmering water, cover and steam for 2–3 minutes until the squid just turns white. Cool under cold running water and drain on paper towels.

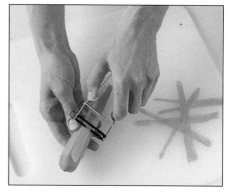

2 Using a swivel-style vegetable peeler, cut the carrot into wafer thin ribbons. Place the lettuce on a serving plate. Sprinkle the carrot ribbons over the top, followed by the diced cucumber.

3 Arrange the mussels, shrimp and squid rings over the salad and sprinkle the capers over the top.

4 Whisk the dressing ingredients in a small bowl and drizzle over the salad. Chill before serving.

Baked Clams

This simple, fresh-tasting tapas also works very well with mussels.

INGREDIENTS

Serves 4

14-ounce can chopped tomatoes
1 red onion, chopped
4 tablespoons chopped fresh chives
1 pound small, fresh clams
1–2 tablespoons olive oil
salt and freshly ground black pepper
chopped chives, to garnish

> ——— COOK'S TIP ———
>
> Cooked this way, the onions are fairly
> crunchy – if you prefer, fry them first.

1 Preheat the oven to 400°F. Turn the tomatoes into a bowl and stir in the chopped onion and chives, with salt and pepper to taste. Transfer to a heat proof dish, cover with foil and bake for 10 minutes.

2 Arrange the clams, joint-side down, in the tomato mixture. Drizzle over the olive oil and return to the oven for 5–10 minutes until the clams have opened. Discard any clams that remain closed, then scatter over the chives and serve immediately.

Spiced Clams

Turmeric is not usually used with clams, but combines with chili powder and fresh ginger to create a delicious dish.

INGREDIENTS

Serves 4

1 small onion, cut into thin wedges
1 celery stalk, sliced
2 garlic cloves, chopped
1-inch piece fresh ginger, grated
2 tablespoons olive oil
1 teaspoon chili powder
1 teaspoon ground turmeric
2 tablespoons chopped fresh parsley
1 pound fresh baby clams
2 tablespoons dry white wine
salt and freshly ground black pepper
celery leaves, to garnish

1 Place the onion, celery, garlic and ginger in a saucepan, add the oil, spices and parsley and stir-fry for 5 minutes.

----- COOK'S TIP -----

It is very important that the paste is cooked for a full 5 minutes or the finished dish will have the harsh taste of raw spices.

2 Add the clams to the pan and cook for 2 minutes.

3 Pour in the wine, then cover and cook gently for 2–3 minutes, shaking the pan occasionally, until all the shells have opened. Add plenty of salt and pepper to taste. Discard any clams whose shells remain closed, then serve immediately, garnished with celery leaves.

Steamed Mussels with Bacon and Beer

The idea of combining mussels, bacon and beer actually comes from Belgium. Surprisingly, these ingredients go remarkably well together and they make a fabulous tapas dish.

INGREDIENTS

Serves 6

1 tablespoon olive oil
1 small onion, chopped
2 garlic cloves, finely chopped
4 rindless smoked lean bacon strips, coarsely chopped
1¼ pounds prepared small mussels
5 tablespoons blond beer or lager
1 teaspoon chopped fresh thyme
coarsely ground black pepper
sprigs of thyme, to garnish

1 Heat the oil in a frying pan and fry the onion, garlic and bacon over high heat for 5 minutes until golden.

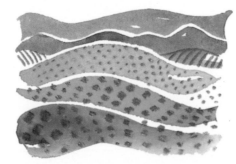

2 Add the mussels, beer or lager and thyme, with pepper to taste. Cover tightly and steam for 3–5 minutes until all the mussels have opened. Spoon into serving dishes, discarding any mussels that remain closed. Serve hot, garnished with thyme sprigs.

Broiled Mussels with Parsley and Parmesan

This is sure to become one of your all-time favorite tapas – as the mussels are broiling, they release an irresistible aroma. When you make them at home, don't be surprised if they are devoured the moment they are ready!

INGREDIENTS

Serves 4

1 pound fresh mussels
3 tablespoons water
1 tablespoon melted butter
1 tablespoon olive oil
3 tablespoons freshly grated
  Parmesan cheese
2 tablespoons chopped fresh parsley
2 garlic cloves, finely chopped
½ teaspoon coarsely ground
  black pepper

2 Place the mussels and water in a large pan. Cover and steam for about 5 minutes, or until the mussels have opened.

3 Drain the mussels, discarding any that remain closed. Snap the top shell off each, leaving the mussel still attached to the bottom shell.

5 Preheat the broiler to high. In a small bowl, mix together the melted butter, olive oil, Parmesan, parsley, garlic and black pepper.

6 Place a small amount of the cheese mixture on top of each mussel.

7 Broil for 2–3 minutes, or until the mussels are sizzling and golden. Serve the mussels in their shells, but remember to give your guests napkins to wipe the juices off their chins!

1 Scrub the mussels thoroughly, scraping off any barnacles with a round-bladed knife and pulling out the gritty beards. Sharply tap any open mussels, and discard any that fail to close.

4 Balance the shells in a casserole, packing them closely together so they stay level.

— COOK'S TIP —

If you can't get fresh mussels, shelled, frozen mussels will work well. Thaw and drain, then place in four individual heat proof dishes. Top with the parsley mixture and broil for the same time. Serve the mussels with teaspoons and offer plenty of bread to mop up the juices.

Broiled Scallops with Brown Butter

This is a very striking dish as the scallops are served on the half shell, still sizzling from the broiler. Reserve it for a special occasion to impress!

INGREDIENTS

Serves 4
¼ cup sweet butter, diced
8 scallops, prepared on the
  half shell
1 tablespoon chopped fresh parsley
salt and freshly ground black pepper
4 lemon wedges, to serve

1 Preheat the broiler to high. Melt the butter in a small saucepan over medium heat until it is pale golden brown. Remove the pan from the heat immediately; the butter must not be allowed to burn.

2 Arrange the scallop shells in a single layer in a casserole or a shallow roasting pan. Brush a little of the brown butter over the scallops and broil for 4 minutes – it will not be necessary to turn them.

3 Pour over the remaining brown butter, then sprinkle a little salt and pepper and the parsley over. Serve immediately, with lemon wedges.

COOK'S TIP

If you can't get hold of scallops in their shells, you can use shelled, fresh scallops if you cook them on the day of purchase.

Fried Squid

The squid is simply dusted in flour and dipped in egg before being fried so the coating is light, and does not mask the flavor.

INGREDIENTS

Serves 4
4 ounces prepared squid, cut
  into rings
2 tablespoons seasoned flour
1 egg
2 tablespoons milk
olive oil, for frying
sea salt
lemon wedges, to serve

COOK'S TIP

For a crisper coating, dust the rings in flour, then dip them in batter instead of this simple egg and flour coating.

1 Toss the squid rings in the seasoned flour in a bowl or strong plastic bag. Beat the egg and milk together in a shallow bowl. Heat the oil in a heavy-bottomed frying pan.

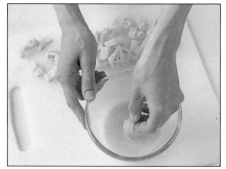

2 Dip the floured squid rings one at a time into the egg mixture, shaking off any excess liquid. Add to the hot oil, in batches if necessary, and fry for 2–3 minutes on each side until golden.

3 Drain the fried squid on paper towels, then sprinkle with salt. Transfer to a small warm plate and serve with the lemon wedges.

Paella Croquettes

Paella is probably Spain's most famous dish, and here it is used for a tasty fried tapas. In this recipe, the paella is cooked from scratch, but you could, of course, use leftover paella instead.

INGREDIENTS

Serves 4

pinch of saffron threads
²/₃ cup white wine
2 tablespoons olive oil
1 small onion, finely chopped
1 garlic clove, finely chopped
²/₃ cup risotto rice
1¼ cups hot chicken stock
2 ounces cooked shrimp, shelled, deveined and coarsely chopped
2 ounces cooked chicken, coarsely chopped
¹/₃ cup petits pois, thawed if frozen
2 tablespoons freshly grated Parmesan cheese
1 egg, beaten
2 tablespoons milk
1½ cups fresh, white bread crumbs
vegetable or olive oil, for frying
salt and freshly ground black pepper
Italian parsley, to garnish

1 Stir the saffron into the wine in a small bowl; set aside.

2 Heat the oil in a saucepan and gently fry the onion and garlic for 5 minutes until softened. Stir in the rice and cook for 1 minute.

3 Keeping the heat fairly high, add the wine and saffron mixture to the pan, stirring until it is all absorbed. Gradually add the stock, stirring until all the liquid has been absorbed and the rice is cooked – this should take about 20 minutes.

--- COOK'S TIP ---

When making paella, it's very important to use a good quality short grain rice. Italian risotto rice, sometimes labeled arborio or carnaroli, works very well.

4 Stir in the shrimp, chicken, petits pois and freshly grated Parmesan. Season to taste with salt and pepper. Let cool slightly, then use two tablespoons to shape the mixture into 16 small lozenges.

5 Mix the egg and milk in a shallow bowl. Spread out the bread crumbs on a sheet of foil. Dip the croquettes in the egg mixture, then coat them in the bread crumbs.

6 Heat the oil in a large frying pan. Shallow fry the croquettes for 4–5 minutes until crisp and golden brown. Drain on paper towels and serve hot, garnished with a sprig of Italian parsley.

FISH TAPAS

This is a rather summery selection of recipes including Broiled Sardines, which are wonderful cooked on a barbecue, and Salt-cured Salmon, which is sliced wafer-thin and served chilled with aïoli. Another European favorite, whitebait, is given a special Spanish feel when fried until crisp and served with a sherry salsa. Also covered in this chapter is the typical Spanish fish bacalao (salt cod) – used here to make two delicious tapas, bite-size fishcakes and basil-flavored fritters.

Monkfish Packages

INGREDIENTS

Serves 4

1½ cups bread flour
2 eggs
4 ounces skinless monkfish fillet, diced
grated rind of 1 lemon
1 garlic clove, chopped
1 small red chili, seeded and sliced
3 tablespoons chopped fresh parsley
2 tablespoons light cream
salt and freshly ground black pepper

For the tomato oil

2 tomatoes, peeled, seeded and
  finely diced
3 tablespoons extra virgin olive oil
1 tablespoon fresh lemon juice

COOK'S TIP

If the dough is sticky, sprinkle a little flour
into the food processor bowl.

1 Place the flour, eggs and ½ teaspoon salt in a food processor, or blender; pulse until it forms a soft dough. Knead for 2–3 minutes. Wrap in plastic wrap and chill for 20 minutes.

2 Place the monkfish, lemon rind, garlic, chili and parsley in the clean food processor; process until very finely chopped. Add the cream, with plenty of salt and pepper, and process again to form a very thick paste.

3 Make the tomato oil by stirring the diced tomatoes with the olive oil and lemon juice in a bowl. Add salt to taste. Cover and chill.

4 Roll out the dough thinly on a lightly floured surface and cut out 32 rounds, using a 1½-inch plain cutter. Divide the filling among half the rounds, then cover with the remaining rounds. Pinch the edges tightly to seal, trying to exclude as much air as possible.

5 Bring a large saucepan of water to a simmer and poach the packages, in batches, for 2–3 minutes, or until they rise to the surface. Drain and serve hot, drizzled with the tomato oil.

Salt Cod Fishcakes with Aïoli

Bite-size fishcakes, dipped in a rich, garlic mayonnaise, are irresistible. Start these in good time, as the salt cod needs lengthy soaking.

INGREDIENTS

Serves 6
1 pound potatoes, peeled and cubed
4 ounces salt cod, soaked in cold water
   for 48 hours
1 tablespoon olive oil
1 small onion, finely chopped
2 garlic cloves, finely chopped
2 tablespoons chopped fresh parsley
1 egg, beaten
Tabasco or chili sauce
all-purpose flour, for dusting
vegetable oil, for frying
salt and freshly ground black pepper
Italian parsley and lemon wedges,
   to garnish
aïoli, to serve

— COOK'S TIP —

Try making these with drained canned fish, such as salmon or tuna.

1 Cook the potatoes in a saucepan of boiling water for 10–12 minutes until tender. Drain well, then mash until smooth. Set aside.

2 Place the cod in a frying pan, add water to cover and bring to a boil. Drain the fish, then remove the skin and bones. Using a fork, break the flesh into small pieces.

3 Heat the olive oil in a small saucepan and cook the onion and garlic for 5 minutes until softened.

4 In a large bowl, mix together the mashed potato, flaked fish, fried onion mixture and parsley. Bind with the egg, then add salt, pepper and Tabasco or chili sauce to taste. With floured hands, shape the mixture into 18 small balls.

5 Flatten the balls slightly and place on a large, floured plate. Chill for about 15 minutes.

6 Heat ½ inch vegetable oil in a large frying pan. Cook the fishcakes for 3–4 minutes on each side until golden. Drain on paper towels and serve hot, with the aïoli, garnished with parsley and lemon wedges.

Salt Cod Fritters

Start this recipe ahead of time as the salt cod must be soaked for 2 days before it is used.

INGREDIENTS

Serves 4–6
1 cup self-rising flour
½ teaspoon salt
1 large egg
4 tablespoons milk
4 ounces salt cod, soaked in water for
    48 hours
4 scallions, finely chopped
handful of basil leaves, coarsely torn
1 teaspoon coarsely ground
    black pepper
olive oil, for frying

1 Sift the flour into a bowl and stir in the salt. Whisk in the egg and milk to make a thick batter.

2 Drain the salt cod. Remove the skin and bones, then flake the flesh. Stir it into the batter with the scallions, basil and pepper.

3 Heat ½ inch olive oil in a frying pan. Place spoonfuls of the mixture into the pan.

4 Cook for 2–3 minutes on each side until puffed and golden. Drain on paper towels and serve hot.

COOK'S TIP

For an extra light result, let the batter rest for 20 minutes before stirring in the scallions, basil and pepper.

Cod with Potato and Mustard Seeds

INGREDIENTS

Serves 4

2 tablespoons olive oil
1 teaspoon mustard seeds
1 large potato, cubed
2 slices of serrano ham, shredded
1 onion, thinly sliced
2 garlic cloves, thinly sliced
1 red chili, seeded and sliced
4 ounces skinless, boneless cod, cubed
½ cup vegetable stock
½ cup grated tasty cheese, such as
   Manchego or Cheddar
salt and freshly ground black pepper

—————— COOK'S TIP ——————

For a crisp topping, substitute half the cheese with whole-wheat bread crumbs.

1 Heat the oil in a heavy-bottomed frying pan. Add the mustard seeds. Cook for a minute or two until the seeds begin to pop and splutter, then add the potato, ham and onion.

2 Cook, stirring regularly for about 10–15 minutes, until the potatoes are brown and almost tender.

3 Add the garlic and chili, and cook for 2 minutes more.

4 Stir in the cod cubes and cook for 2–3 minutes until white, then add the stock and plenty of salt and pepper. Cover the pan and cook for 5 minutes, until the fish is just cooked and the potatoes are tender.

5 Transfer the mixture to a casserole. Sprinkle over the grated cheese and place under a hot broiler for about 2–3 minutes until the cheese is golden and bubbling.

Fried Whitebait with Sherry Salsa

INGREDIENTS

Serves 4
8 ounces whitebait, thawed if frozen
2 tablespoons seasoned flour
4 tablespoons olive oil
4 tablespoons vegetable oil

For the salsa
1 shallot, finely chopped
2 garlic cloves, finely chopped
4 ripe tomatoes, coarsely chopped
1 small red chili, seeded and finely
   chopped
2 tablespoons olive oil
4 tablespoons sweet sherry
2–3 tablespoons chopped fresh herbs,
   such as basil, parsley or cilantro
½ cup fresh, white bread crumbs
salt and freshly ground black pepper

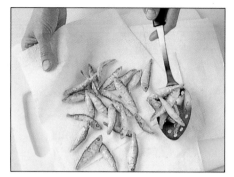

1 To make the salsa, place the shallot, garlic, tomatoes, chili and oil in a pan. Cover with a lid and cook gently for 10 minutes.

2 Pour in the sherry and add salt and pepper to taste. Stir in the herbs and bread crumbs, then cover and keep hot until the whitebait are ready.

3 Wash the whitebait thoroughly, drain well, then dust in the seasoned flour to coat. Heat both oils together in a heavy-bottomed frying pan and cook the fish in batches until crisp and golden. Drain on paper towels and keep warm in a low oven until all the fish are cooked. Serve immediately with the salsa.

Crispy Fish Balls

You can use any white fish to make these crispy balls. Cod, haddock and monkfish fillet all work well.

INGREDIENTS

Serves 6
1 egg
pinch of saffron threads
2 garlic cloves, coarsely chopped
3 tablespoons parsley leaves
8 ounces white fish, skinned, boned
   and cubed
3 ounces white bread,
   crusts removed
4 tablespoons seasoned flour
vegetable oil, for frying
salt and freshly ground black pepper
lemon wedges and mayonnaise,
   to serve

1 Beat the egg and saffron threads together in a cup, then set aside for 5 minutes.

2 In a food processor or blender, process the garlic and parsley until finely chopped. Add the fish and bread and process until they are well blended. Scrape the fish mixture into a bowl and stir in the egg and saffron. Season with plenty of salt and pepper.

3 Shape the mixture into 24 small balls. Spread out the seasoned flour in a shallow dish and coat the balls on all sides.

4 Heat the oil in a deep frying pan. Fry the fish balls, in batches if necessary, until crisp and golden, shaking the pan to keep them moving. Drain on paper towels and serve immediately with lemon wedges. Offer a small bowl of mayonnaise for dipping and toothpicks for spearing.

Broiled Sardines

Fresh sardines have plenty of flavor, so they are at their best when cooked simply.

Ingredients

Serves 4

8 sardines, about 2 ounces each
sea salt
2 lemons, halved

1 Gut the sardines, but leave on the heads and tails. Slash each of the sardines' sides diagonally three times.

2 Preheat the broiler to high. Place the sardines on a rack and sprinkle with sea salt. Broil for 4 minutes on each side until the flesh is cooked and the skin is blistered and a little charred.

3 Transfer to a serving dish and serve immediately with the lemon halves to squeeze over.

Salt-cured Salmon

Ingredients

Serves 10

¼ cup sea salt
3 tablespoons superfine sugar
1 teaspoon chili powder
1 teaspoon coarsely ground
  black pepper
3 tablespoons chopped fresh cilantro
2 x 9-ounce salmon fillets
Italian parsley, to garnish
aïoli, to serve

— Cook's Tip —

Make the most of the leftover salmon skin by turning it into delicious, crunchy strips: after slicing the salt-cured salmon, scrape any remaining fish off the skin and discard. Cut the skin into ½-inch wide strips. Fry for 1 minute in hot oil until crisp and browned. Drain on paper towels and let cool. Serve as a garnish for the salt-cured salmon, or as a tapas dish in its own right.

3 Chill for 48 hours, turning every 8 hours or so and basting with the liquid that forms in the dish.

1 In a bowl, mix together the salt, sugar, chili powder, pepper and cilantro. Rub the mixture into the flesh of each salmon fillet.

2 Place one of the fillets, skin-side down, in a shallow glass dish. Place the other fillet on top, with the skin-side up. Cover with foil, then place a weight on top.

4 Drain the salmon well and transfer to a board. Using a sharp knife, slice it diagonally into wafer-thin slices. Arrange on plates and garnish with sprigs of parsley. Serve with the aïoli.

MEAT AND POULTRY TAPAS

This chapter includes a mixture of authentic tapas, such as Chorizo in Red Wine, and Spicy Meatballs, along with delicious contemporary dishes, such as Chicken with Lemon and Garlic, and Ham and Cheese Toasts, which are made using traditional ingredients. Sausages, including morcilla, fresh, spicy sausages and cured chorizo sausage, all feature strongly, with recipes for the popular tapas dish, Fried Black Pudding, and a robust Sausage Stew.

Pastry-wrapped Chorizo Puffs

These flaky pastry puffs, filled with spicy chorizo sausage and grated cheese, make a perfect accompaniment to a glass of cold sherry or beer. You can use any type of hard cheese for the puffs, but for best results, choose a mild variety, as the chorizo has plenty of flavor.

INGREDIENTS

Serves 8

8 ounces puff pastry, thawed
  if frozen
4 ounces cured chorizo sausage,
  chopped
½ cup grated cheese
1 small egg, beaten
1 teaspoon paprika

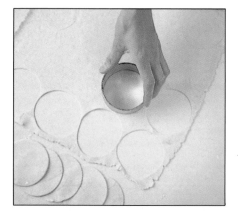

1 Roll out the pastry thinly on a floured surface. Using a 3-inch cutter, stamp out as many rounds as possible, then re-roll the trimmings, if necessary, and stamp out more rounds to make 16 in all.

2 Preheat the oven to 450°F. Put the chopped chorizo sausage and grated cheese in a bowl and toss together lightly.

3 Lay one of the pastry rounds on the palm of your hand and place a little of the chorizo mixture across the center.

4 Using your other hand, pinch the edges of the pastry together along the top to seal, as when making a miniature patty. Repeat the process with the remaining rounds to make 16 puffs in all.

COOK'S TIP

Prepare the chorizo puffs a day or two ahead, if you like. Chill them without the glaze, wrapped in a plastic bag, until ready to bake, then let them come back to room temperature while you preheat the oven.

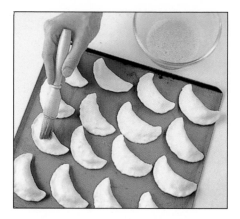

5 Place the pastries on a nonstick baking sheet and brush lightly with the beaten egg. Using a small sifter or tea strainer, dust the tops lightly with a little of the paprika.

6 Bake the pastries in the oven for 10–12 minutes, until puffed and golden brown. Transfer the pastries to a wire rack and let cool for 5 minutes, then serve warm, dusted with the remaining paprika.

Chorizo in Red Wine

This simple dish is flamed just before serving. If you wish, use small chorizo sausages and leave them whole. Provide toothpicks for spearing the chorizo.

INGREDIENTS

Serves 4
8 ounces cured chorizo sausage
6 tablespoons red wine
2 tablespoons brandy
chopped fresh parsley, to garnish

***

COOK'S TIP

After cooking in the wine, the chorizo can be cooled, then chilled for up to 24 hours.

***

1 Prick the chorizo sausage(s) in several places with a fork, and place in a pan with the wine. Bring to a boil, lower the heat, then cover and simmer gently for 15 minutes. Remove from the heat and let cool in the covered pan for 2 hours.

2 Remove the chorizo sausage(s) from the pan and reserve the wine.

3 Cut the chorizo sausage(s) into ½-inch slices.

4 Heat the chorizo in a heavy-bottomed frying pan, then pour over the brandy and light very carefully with a match. When the flames have died down, add the reserved wine and cook for 2–3 minutes until piping hot. Serve garnished with chopped parsley.

Fried Black Pudding

Black pudding (*morcilla*) is a very popular tapas dish. In Spain the sausage is often homemade.

INGREDIENTS

Serves 4

1 tablespoon olive oil
1 onion, thinly sliced
2 garlic cloves, thinly sliced
1 teaspoon dried oregano or marjoram
1 teaspoon paprika
8 ounces black pudding, cut in
   12 thick slices
1 small French stick, sliced into
   12 rounds
2 tablespoons dry sherry
sugar, to taste
salt and freshly ground black pepper
chopped oregano, to garnish

1 Heat the oil in a large frying pan and fry the onion, garlic, oregano and paprika for 7–8 minutes until the onion is softened and golden.

2 Add the black pudding slices, raise the heat and cook for 3 minutes on each side until crisp.

3 Arrange the rounds of bread on a large serving plate and top each with a slice of black pudding. Stir the sherry into the mixture remaining in the frying pan, with sugar to taste. Heat, swirling around until bubbling, then season with salt and pepper.

4 Spoon a little of the onion mixture on top of each slice of black pudding. Sprinkle the oregano over the top and serve immediately.

COOK'S TIP

If you do find real *morcilla*, which is usually flavored with spices and herbs (including paprika, garlic and marjoram), serve it neat: simply fry the slices in olive oil and use to top little rounds of bread.

Sausage Stew

This robust tapas dish is very good served with a glass of beer.

INGREDIENTS

Serves 4
1 tablespoon olive oil
1 onion, chopped
2 garlic cloves, finely chopped
1 carrot, chopped
4 fresh, spicy sausages
²/₃ cup tomato juice
1 tablespoon brandy
¼ teaspoon Tabasco sauce
1 teaspoon sugar
salt and freshly ground black pepper
2 tablespoons chopped fresh cilantro,
    to garnish

1 Heat the oil in a large saucepan. Cook the onion, garlic, carrot and sausages for 10 minutes, stirring occasionally until evenly browned.

2 Stir in the tomato juice, brandy, Tabasco and sugar, with salt and pepper to taste. Cover and simmer for 25 minutes until the sausages are cooked through and the sauce has thickened. Serve immediately, garnished with chopped cilantro.

Stewed Beans and Pork

Fabada is a classic Spanish stew that takes its name from a type of white bean. It always contains black pudding (*morcilla*) and chorizo sausage and usually takes a good 2 hours to prepare. Here is a simple, speedy version that serves very well as tapas.

INGREDIENTS

Serves 4
1 tablespoon olive oil
6 ounces belly pork, rind removed
    and diced
4 ounces cured chorizo sausage, diced
1 onion, chopped
2 garlic cloves, finely chopped
1 large tomato, coarsely chopped
¼ teaspoon dried chili flakes
14-ounce can cannellini beans, drained
²/₃ cup chicken stock
salt and freshly ground black pepper
Italian parsley, to garnish

1 Heat the oil in a large frying pan and fry the pork, chorizo, onion and garlic for 5–10 minutes until the onion has softened and browned. Add the tomato and chili flakes and cook for 1 minute more.

2 Stir in the beans and stock. Bring to a boil, lower the heat, cover and simmer for 15–20 minutes until the pork is cooked through. Add salt and pepper to taste and serve, garnished with parsley.

— COOK'S TIP —

If preferred, smoked ham can be used in place of belly pork in this recipe. Although it isn't quite as authentic, the meat is a lot less fatty and it adds a good, smoky flavor to the stew.

Barbecued Mini Ribs

These tasty ribs are delicious barbecued and almost as good when broiled.

INGREDIENTS

Serves 6–8

1 sheet of pork ribs, about 1½ pounds
6 tablespoons sweet sherry
1 tablespoon tomato paste
1 teaspoon soy sauce
½ teaspoon Tabasco sauce
1 tablespoon light brown sugar
2 tablespoons seasoned flour
coarse sea salt

— COOK'S TIP —

Use freshly squeezed orange juice instead of sherry for a sweeter flavor.

1 Separate the ribs, then, using a heavy knife, cut each rib in half widthwise to make about 30 pieces.

2 Mix the sherry, tomato paste, soy sauce, Tabasco and sugar in a bowl. Stir in ½ teaspoon salt.

3 Toss the ribs in the seasoned flour in a strong plastic bag, then dip each rib separately in the sherry sauce. Arrange the ribs on a broiler tray and cook over hot coals or under a hot broiler for 30–40 minutes until cooked through and a little charred. Sprinkle with sea salt and serve immediately.

Ham and Cheese Toasts

These crunchy toasts are extremely simple to make and can be prepared and cooked in just a couple of minutes – perfect for unexpected guests or an impromptu snack.

INGREDIENTS

Serves 4

1 small French stick, sliced into 12 rounds
1 large garlic clove, peeled
3 slices of salt-cured ham, such as serrano or prosciutto, quartered
½ cup grated cheese, such as Manchego or Cheddar
coarse black pepper

1 Toast the bread under a hot broiler until both sides are golden brown. Cut the garlic clove in half and rub the cut surfaces over one side of each piece of toast.

2 Place the ham on top of the garlic-flavored toasts. Ripple the ham so that it fits loosely on the toast round.

3 Top each toast with grated cheese, then sprinkle with the pepper. Return to the broiler and cook for about 1–2 minutes until the cheese is bubbling and the edges of the toasts are slightly charred. Serve hot.

— COOK'S TIP —

Use other crusty bread, or cut 2-inch squares of thick-cut sliced bread and substitute for the French stick for this dish.

Cheese and Ham Potato Patties

These soft patties can be served hot or cold – for a real treat, top each with a fried quail egg.

INGREDIENTS

Serves 4
1¼ pounds potatoes, peeled
   and cubed
2 tablespoons butter
¼ cup grated cheese, such as Manchego
   or aged Cheddar
4 slices of serrano ham, chopped
½ cup all-purpose flour
oil for greasing
salt and freshly ground black pepper

1 Cook the potatoes in a saucepan of boiling, lightly salted water for 10–15 minutes until tender. Drain well and mash with the butter and cheese until smooth.

2 Stir in the ham and flour with plenty of salt and pepper. Shape the mixture into eight rounds, each about ½ inch thick.

3 Lightly oil a griddle or heavy-bottomed frying pan and cook the patties for 4–5 minutes on each side until golden brown. Drain on paper towels and serve immediately.

— COOK'S TIP —

The patties have a very fluffy, soft center, so take care when turning them over. If preferred, brush them with oil and cook them under a moderately hot broiler, turning them halfway through cooking.

Egg-fried Ham Sandwiches

For a new slant on the toasted sandwich, serve these tasty snacks with their golden egg coating. Vary the filling – cheese works especially well.

INGREDIENTS

Serves 2
2 slices of serrano ham
2 large slices of white bread, crusts removed
1 egg
2 tablespoons milk
2 tablespoons olive oil
coarse sea salt and freshly ground black pepper

───── COOK'S TIP ─────

The longer you soak the sandwich, the more egg mixture will be absorbed and the lighter and fluffier will be the result – 15 minutes is ideal.

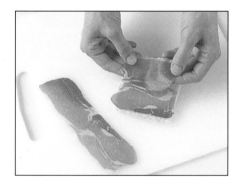

1 Lay both slices of ham on one of the slices of bread. Sprinkle with pepper, then cover with the other slice of bread to make a sandwich.

2 Beat the egg and milk together in a shallow dish. Cut the sandwich into four squares and place in the egg mixture, turning once or twice until all the liquid has been absorbed.

3 Heat the oil in a frying pan. Cook the sandwiches for 3–4 minutes on each side until puffed up and golden brown. Remove with a fish slice and drain on paper towels. Sprinkle lightly with sea salt and serve hot.

Spicy Meatballs

These meatballs are delicious served piping hot with chili sauce on the side, so guests can add as much heat as they like.

INGREDIENTS

Serves 6

4 ounces fresh, spicy sausages
4 ounces ground beef
2 shallots, finely chopped
2 garlic cloves, finely chopped
1½ cups fresh, white bread crumbs
1 egg, beaten
2 tablespoons chopped fresh parsley, plus extra to garnish
1 tablespoon olive oil
salt and freshly ground black pepper
Tabasco sauce or other hot chili sauce, to serve

1 Remove the skins from the sausages and place the sausage meat in a small mixing bowl.

— COOK'S TIP —

If you like, you can make the meatballs up to a day in advance, then cover and chill them until ready to cook.

2 Add the ground beef, shallots, garlic, bread crumbs, beaten egg and parsley, with plenty of salt and pepper. Mix well, then shape into 18 small balls.

3 Heat the olive oil in a frying pan and cook the meatballs, in batches if necessary, for 15–20 minutes, stirring regularly until evenly browned and cooked through.

4 Transfer the meatballs to a warm plate and sprinkle with chopped parsley. Serve with chili sauce. Offer toothpicks for spearing.

Meatballs in Tomato Sauce

Serve this traditional tapas dish with crusty bread and a robust red wine or, for a light meal for two, with a bowl of steaming pasta tossed in olive oil.

INGREDIENTS

Serves 4
8 ounces ground beef or lamb
4 scallions, thinly sliced
2 garlic cloves, finely chopped
2 tablespoons freshly grated Parmesan
2 teaspoons fresh thyme leaves
1 tablespoon olive oil
3 tomatoes, chopped
2 tablespoons red or dry white wine
2 teaspoons chopped fresh rosemary
pinch of sugar
salt and freshly ground black pepper
fresh thyme, to garnish

1 Place the ground beef or lamb in a bowl. Add the scallions, garlic, Parmesan and thyme and plenty of salt and pepper.

2 Mix well, then shape the mixture into 12 small, firm balls.

3 Heat the olive oil in a large frying pan and cook the meatballs for 5 minutes, turning frequently until evenly browned.

4 Add the chopped tomatoes, wine, rosemary and sugar, with salt and pepper to taste. Cover and cook gently for 15 minutes until the tomatoes are pulpy and the meatballs are cooked. Serve hot, garnished with thyme.

Spicy Chicken Wings

These deliciously sticky bites will appeal to adults and children alike, although younger eaters might prefer a little less chili.

INGREDIENTS

Serves 4

8 plump chicken wings
2 large garlic cloves, cut into slivers
1 tablespoon olive oil
1 tablespoon paprika
1 teaspoon chili powder
1 teaspoon dried oregano
1 teaspoon salt
1 teaspoon ground black pepper
lime wedges, to serve

> ——— COOK'S TIP ———
>
> Chunks of chicken breast and small thighs may also be cooked in this way.

1 Using a small, sharp knife, make one or two cuts in the skin of each chicken wing and carefully slide a sliver of garlic under the skin. Brush the wings with the olive oil.

2 In a large bowl, stir together the paprika, chili powder, oregano, salt and pepper. Add the chicken wings and toss together until very lightly coated in the mixture.

3 Broil or barbecue the chicken wings for 15 minutes until they are cooked through with a blackened, crispy skin. Serve with lime wedges to squeeze over.

Chicken with Lemon and Garlic

Extremely easy to cook and delicious to eat, serve this succulent tapas dish with fried potatoes and aïoli.

INGREDIENTS

Serves 4

8 ounces skinless chicken breast fillets
2 tablespoons olive oil
1 shallot, finely chopped
4 garlic cloves, finely chopped
1 teaspoon paprika
juice of 1 lemon
2 tablespoons chopped fresh parsley
salt and freshly ground black pepper
Italian parsley, to garnish
lemon wedges, to serve

1 Sandwich the chicken breast fillets between two sheets of plastic wrap or wax paper. Beat out evenly with a rolling pin until the fillets are about ¼ inch thick.

> ——— COOK'S TIP ———
>
> For a variation on this dish, try using strips of turkey breast or pork.

2 Cut the chicken into strips about ½ inch wide. Heat the oil in a large frying pan. Stir-fry the chicken strips with the shallot, garlic and paprika over high heat for about 3 minutes until lightly browned and cooked through. Add the lemon juice and parsley with salt and pepper to taste. Serve hot with lemon wedges, garnished with parsley.

Chicken Liver Pâté

This rich-tasting, smooth pâté will keep in the fridge for about 3 days. Serve with thick slices of hot toast or warm bread – a rustic olive oil bread such as ciabatta would be ideal.

INGREDIENTS

Serves 8

4 ounces chicken livers, thawed if
   frozen, trimmed
1 small garlic clove, chopped
1 tablespoon sherry
2 tablespoons brandy
¼ cup butter, melted
¼ teaspoon salt
fresh herbs and black peppercorns,
   to garnish
hot toast or warm bread, to serve

1 Preheat the oven to 300°F. Place the chicken livers and chopped garlic in a food processor or blender and process until smooth.

2 With the motor running, gradually add the sherry, brandy, melted butter and salt.

3 Pour the mixture into two 3-inch ramekins and cover with foil.

4 Place the ramekins in a small roasting pan and pour in boiling water until it comes halfway up the sides of the ramekins.

5 Carefully transfer the pan to the oven and bake for 20 minutes. Let cool to room temperature, then remove the ramekins from the pan and chill until ready to serve. Serve the pâté with toast or bread, garnished with herbs and peppercorns.

Chicken Croquettes

This recipe comes from Rebato's, a tapas bar in London. The chef there makes croquettes with a number of flavorings; this version uses chicken.

INGREDIENTS

Serves 4
2 tablespoons butter
¼ cup all-purpose flour
⅔ cup milk
1 tablespoon olive oil
1 boneless chicken breast with skin, about 3 ounces, diced
1 garlic clove, finely chopped
1 small egg, beaten
1 cup fresh, white bread crumbs
vegetable oil, for deep-frying
salt and freshly ground black pepper
Italian parsley, to garnish
lemon wedges, to serve

1 Melt the butter in a small saucepan. Add the flour and cook gently, stirring, for 1 minute. Gradually beat in the milk to make a smooth, very thick sauce. Cover with a lid and remove from the heat.

2 Heat the oil in a frying pan and cook the chicken with the garlic for 5 minutes, until the chicken is lightly browned and cooked through.

3 Turn the contents of the frying pan into a food processor or blender and process until finely chopped. Stir into the sauce. Add plenty of salt and pepper to taste. Let cool completely.

4 Shape into eight small sausages, then dip each in egg and then bread crumbs. Deep-fry in hot oil for 4 minutes until crisp and golden. Drain on paper towels and serve with lemon wedges, garnished with parsley.

Chicken Livers in Sherry

This dish makes an excellent addition to any tapas spread. Serve with crusty bread.

INGREDIENTS

Serves 4
8 ounces chicken livers, thawed if
   frozen, trimmed
1 small onion
2 small garlic cloves
1 tablespoon olive oil
1 teaspoon fresh thyme leaves
2 tablespoons sweet sherry
2 tablespoons sour or heavy cream
salt and freshly ground black pepper
fresh thyme, to garnish

1 Trim any green spots and sinews from the chicken livers; set aside while you prepare the onion and garlic.

2 Finely chop the onion and garlic using a sharp knife.

3 Heat the oil in a frying pan and fry the onion, garlic, chicken livers and thyme for 3 minutes.

4 Stir in the sherry and cook gently for 1 minute. Add the sour or heavy cream and cook over low heat for 1–2 minutes more. Stir in salt and pepper to taste and serve immediately, garnished with thyme.

Sweet Crust Lamb

These little noisettes are just big enough for two mouthfuls, so are ideal for tapas. If you would prefer something a little more substantial, small lamb cutlets or chops can be prepared in the same way.

INGREDIENTS

Serves 8

6 ounces tender lamb fillet, sliced into ½-inch rounds
1 teaspoon English mustard
2 tablespoons light brown sugar
salt and freshly ground black pepper
toothpicks, to serve

1 Preheat the broiler to high. Sprinkle the lamb generously with salt and pepper and broil on one side for 2 minutes until well browned.

2 Remove the broiler tray from the broiler. Turn the lamb rounds over and spread with the mustard.

3 Sprinkle the sugar evenly over the lamb rounds, then return the broiler tray to the broiler.

4 Cook the lamb for 2–3 minutes more, until the sugar has melted, but the lamb is still pink in the center. Serve with toothpicks for spearing.

COOK'S TIP

Watch the lamb carefully while it is broiling, as the sugar may burn if cooked for more than a few minutes.

Skewered Lamb with Red Onion Salsa

This summery tapas dish is ideal for outdoor eating, although, if the weather fails, the skewers can be cooked under a conventional broiler. The simple salsa makes a refreshing accompaniment – make sure that you use a mild-flavored red onion that is fresh and crisp, and a tomato which is ripe and full of flavor.

INGREDIENTS

Serves 4

8 ounces lean lamb, cubed
½ teaspoon ground cumin
1 teaspoon paprika
1 tablespoon olive oil
salt and freshly ground black pepper

For the salsa

1 red onion, very thinly sliced
1 large tomato, seeded and chopped
1 tablespoon red wine vinegar
3–4 fresh basil or mint leaves,
   coarsely torn
small mint leaves, to garnish

1 Place the lamb in a bowl with the cumin, paprika, olive oil and plenty of salt and pepper. Toss well until the lamb is coated with spices.

2 Cover the bowl with plastic wrap and let rest in a cool place for a few hours, or in the fridge overnight, so that the lamb absorbs the flavors.

3 Spear the lamb cubes on four small skewers – if using wooden skewers, soak first in cold water for 30 minutes to prevent them from burning.

4 To make the salsa, put the sliced onion, tomato, vinegar and basil or mint leaves in a small bowl and stir together until thoroughly blended. Season to taste with salt, garnish with mint, then set aside while you cook the skewered lamb.

5 Cook the skewered lamb over hot coals or under a preheated broiler for about 5–10 minutes, turning the skewers frequently, until the lamb is well browned but still slightly pink in the center. Serve hot, with the salsa.

COOK'S TIP

For an alternative to the red onion salsa, stir chopped fresh mint or basil and a little lemon juice into a small pot of plain, strained yogurt. Drizzle the mixture over the cooked kebabs before serving.

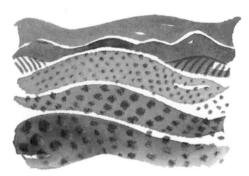

VEGETARIAN AND VEGETABLE TAPAS

When presenting a selection of tapas, it is important to balance out the meat and seafood dishes with a few vegetable tapas – many of which are the more well known, such as tortilla and patatas bravas. Although most fresh vegetables are available all year round, try to choose vegetables when in the peak of the season as they are not only less expensive but also far more flavorsome – very important for dishes such as Tomato and Garlic Bread. This chapter also includes other non-meat dishes such as Fried Cheese and Fried Dough Balls.

Mini Rice Omelets

INGREDIENTS

Serves 4
2 tablespoons olive oil
1 cup cooked white rice
1 potato, grated
4 scallions, thinly sliced
1 garlic clove, finely chopped
1 tablespoon chopped fresh parsley
3 eggs, beaten
salt and freshly ground black pepper

1 Heat half the oil in a large frying pan and stir-fry the rice, with the potato, scallions and garlic, over high heat for 3 minutes until golden.

2 Turn the rice and vegetable mixture into a bowl and stir in the parsley and eggs, with plenty of salt and pepper. Mix well.

3 Heat the remaining oil in the frying pan and drop in large spoonfuls of the rice mixture, leaving room for spreading. Cook the omelets for 1–2 minutes on one side, then flip over and cook the other side.

4 Drain the omelets on paper towels and keep hot while cooking the remaining mixture to make eight small omelets in all. Serve hot.

Fried Cheese

This tapas works very well with Cheddar, mozzarella and, surprisingly, goat cheese, but the best is Manchego. This dish doesn't like to wait around, so fill your kitchen with friends who are ready to eat the cubes as soon as they're out of the pan.

INGREDIENTS

Serves 4
8 ounces firm cheese
2 tablespoons seasoned flour
1 egg, beaten
4 tablespoons chopped fresh dill
vegetable oil, for frying

1 Cut the cheese into ¾-inch cubes. Roll the cubes in seasoned flour to coat them evenly.

2 Beat the egg and dill together, then dip the cubes into the mixture to coat. Heat 1 inch oil in a heavy-bottomed frying pan. Fry the cubes for 1–2 minutes on each side until golden.

3 Remove the cubes with a slotted spoon, drain on paper towels and serve immediately, with toothpicks on hand for spearing.

> ——— COOK'S TIP ———
>
> Test the temperature with one cube of cheese before you cook them all. If the oil is not hot enough, the cheese will take too long to crisp and the center is likely to ooze out completely.

Cheese Puff Balls

INGREDIENTS

Serves 4

4 tablespoons butter, cubed
¼ teaspoon salt
1 cup water
1 cup all-purpose flour
2 whole eggs, plus 1 yolk
½ teaspoon English mustard
    powder
½ teaspoon cayenne pepper
½ cup finely grated well-flavored
    cheese, such as Manchego
        or Cheddar

—— COOK'S TIP ——

Stir chopped chives, smoked salmon or
ham into cream cheese and use as a filling
for cold puffs.

1 Preheat the oven to 425°F. Place
the butter, salt and water in a pan.
Bring to a boil.

2 Sift the flour onto a large sheet
of wax paper, then turn it into the
boiling liquid all at once and stir in
very quickly.

3 Beat the mixture with a wooden
spoon to form a thick paste that
leaves the sides of the pan clean.
Remove the pan from the heat.

4 Beat in the eggs and yolk, one at a
time, then add the mustard,
cayenne and cheese.

5 Place teaspoonfuls of the mixture
onto a nonstick baking sheet and
bake for 10 minutes. Lower the oven
temperature to 350°F and cook for
15 minutes more until well browned.
Serve immediately, or cool on a wire
rack and serve cold.

Tomato and Garlic Bread

A basket of warm, crusty, garlic-flavored bread is a compulsory addition to any tapas table.

INGREDIENTS

Serves 4–6
4 large, ripe tomatoes,
  coarsely chopped
2 garlic cloves, roughly chopped
¼ teaspoon sea salt
grated rind and juice of ½ lemon
1 teaspoon light brown sugar
1 flat loaf of bread, such as ciabatta
2 tablespoons olive oil
freshly ground black pepper

1 Preheat the oven to 400°F. Place the tomatoes, garlic, salt, lemon rind and brown sugar in a small saucepan. Cover and cook gently for 5 minutes until the tomatoes have released their juices and the mixture is quite watery.

2 Split the loaf in half horizontally, then cut each half widthwise into two or three pieces. Place on a baking sheet and bake for 5–8 minutes until hot, crisp and golden brown.

3 While the bread is baking, stir the lemon juice and olive oil into the tomato mixture. Cook uncovered for 8 minutes more, until the mixture is thick and pulpy.

4 Spread the tomato mixture on the hot bread, sprinkle with pepper and serve immediately.

Fried Dough Balls with Fiery Salsa

These crunchy dough balls are accompanied by a hot and spicy tomato salsa. Serve them with a juicy tomato salad, if you prefer.

INGREDIENTS

Serves 10

4 cups white bread flour
1 teaspoon fast-rising dried yeast
1 teaspoon salt
2 tablespoons chopped fresh parsley
2 garlic cloves, finely chopped
2 tablespoons olive oil, plus extra
   for greasing
vegetable oil, for frying

For the salsa

6 hot red chilies, seeded and
   coarsely chopped
1 onion, coarsely chopped
2 garlic cloves, quartered
1-inch piece fresh ginger,
   coarsely chopped
1 pound tomatoes, coarsely chopped
2 tablespoons olive oil
pinch of sugar
salt and freshly ground black pepper

1 Sift the flour into a large bowl. Stir in the yeast and salt and make a well in the center. Add the parsley, garlic, olive oil and enough warm water to make a firm dough.

2 Gather the dough in the bowl together, then turn out onto a lightly floured surface or board. Knead for about 10 minutes, until the dough feels very smooth and elastic.

3 Rub a little oil into the surface of the dough. Return it to the clean bowl, cover with plastic wrap or a clean dish towel and let rise in a warm place for about 1 hour, or until doubled in bulk.

4 Meanwhile, make the salsa. Combine the chilies, onion, garlic and ginger in a food processor or blender and process together until very finely chopped. Add the tomatoes and olive oil, and process until smooth.

5 Strain the mixture into a saucepan. Add sugar, salt and pepper to taste and simmer gently for 15 minutes. Do not allow the salsa to boil.

6 Roll the dough into about 40 balls. Shallow fry in batches in hot oil for 4–5 minutes until crisp and golden. Drain on paper towels and serve hot, with the fiery salsa in a separate bowl for dipping.

COOK'S TIP

These dough balls can be deep-fried for 3–4 minutes or baked at 400°F for 15–20 minutes.

Broiled Bell Pepper Tartlets

INGREDIENTS

Serves 4

1½ cups all-purpose flour
pinch of salt
6 tablespoons chilled butter, diced
2 – 3 tablespoons water
1 red bell pepper, seeded and quartered
1 yellow bell pepper, seeded and
  quartered
4 tablespoons heavy cream
1 egg
1 tablespoon freshly grated Parmesan
salt and freshly ground black pepper

— COOK'S TIP —

For a change, try filling the pastry cases
with strips of broiled eggplant mixed with
sun-dried tomato, or strips of broiled
zucchini mixed with toasted pine nuts.

1 Sift the flour and salt into a bowl. Add the butter and work it in with your fingertips until the mixture resembles fine bread crumbs. Stir in enough water to make a firm, not sticky, dough.

2 Preheat the oven to 400°F. Roll the dough out thinly on a lightly floured surface and line 12 individual molds or a 12-hole muffin pan. Prick the bases with a fork and fill the pastry shells with crumpled foil. Bake for 10 minutes.

3 Meanwhile, place the bell peppers skin-side up on a baking sheet and broil for 10 minutes until the skin is blistered and blackened. Cover with a dish towel and let stand for 5 minutes, then peel away the skin.

4 Cut each piece of bell pepper lengthwise into very thin strips. Remove the foil from the pastry shells and divide the bell pepper strips among the pastry shells.

5 Whisk the cream and egg in a bowl. Add plenty of salt and pepper and pour over the bell peppers. Sprinkle the Parmesan over each filled tartlet and bake for 15 – 20 minutes until firm and golden brown. Cool for 2 minutes before removing from the molds. Transfer to wire racks and serve warm or cold.

Baked Bell Peppers and Tomatoes

Make sure there is plenty of warm crusty bread on hand to serve with this dish so that none of the delicious cooking juices are wasted.

INGREDIENTS

Serves 8
2 red bell peppers
2 yellow bell peppers
1 red onion, sliced
2 garlic cloves, halved
6 plum tomatoes, quartered
¼ cup black olives
1 teaspoon light brown sugar
3 tablespoons sherry
3–4 rosemary sprigs
2 tablespoons olive oil
salt and freshly ground black pepper

1 Seed the bell peppers, then cut each into 12 strips.

2 Preheat the oven to 400°F. Place the bell peppers, onion, garlic, tomatoes and olives in a large roasting pan. Sprinkle over the sugar, then pour over the sherry. Season well, cover with foil and bake for 45 minutes.

3 Remove the foil from the pan and stir the mixture well. Add the rosemary sprigs.

4 Drizzle over the olive oil. Return the pan to the oven for 30 minutes more until the vegetables are tender. Serve hot.

COOK'S TIP

Use four or five well-flavored beefsteak tomatoes instead of plum tomatoes, if you prefer. Cut them into thick wedges instead of quarters.

Fried Spinach with Garlic

Serve this dish warm, or chill and squeeze over a little lemon juice just before eating.

INGREDIENTS

Serves 4
2 tomatoes
1 pound spinach
2 garlic cloves, very thinly sliced
3 tablespoons olive oil
salt and grated nutmeg

COOK'S TIP

There are a number of easy ways to remove the skin from a tomato – if you don't have a gas stove, place the tomatoes under a hot broiler for 1 minute on each side, or plunge them into a saucepan of boiling water for 1 minute.

1 Spear each tomato in turn on a fork and hold in the flame of a gas burner for a few seconds on each side until the skin blisters (see Cook's Tip). Peel off the skin, cut the tomatoes in half, scoop out the seeds and discard.

2 Chop the flesh of the tomatoes into ¼-inch pieces.

3 Wash the spinach well. Place it in a large saucepan with the chopped tomatoes and the garlic. Cover and steam for 5 minutes until dark green and wilted. Drain well.

4 Heat the olive oil in a large frying pan. Gently fry the spinach mixture, tossing and turning until it is glossy and hot. Do not let the garlic darken, or it will taste bitter. Season the spinach and serve, sprinkled with a little grated nutmeg.

Charred Artichokes with Lemon Oil Dip

INGREDIENTS

Serves 4

1 tablespoon lemon juice or
  wine vinegar
2 artichokes, trimmed
12 garlic cloves, unpeeled
3 tablespoons olive oil
1 lemon
3 tablespoons olive oil
sea salt
sprigs of Italian parsley,
  to garnish

1 Preheat the oven to 400°F. Add the lemon juice or vinegar to a bowl of cold water. Cut each artichoke lengthwise into wedges. Pull the hairy choke out from the center of each wedge, then drop them into the acidulated water.

2 Drain the artichoke wedges and place in a roasting pan with the garlic. Add the oil and toss well to coat. Sprinkle with salt and roast for 40 minutes, stirring once or twice, until they are tender and a little charred.

3 Meanwhile, make the dip. Using a small, sharp knife thinly pare away two strips of rind from the lemon. Lay the strips of rind on a board and carefully scrape away any remaining pith. Place the rind in a small pan with water to cover. Bring to a boil, then simmer for 5 minutes. Drain the rind, refresh it in cold water, then chop it coarsely. Set it aside.

4 Arrange the cooked artichokes on a serving plate and set aside to cool for 5 minutes. Using the back of a fork, gently flatten the garlic cloves so that the flesh squeezes out of the skins. Transfer the garlic flesh to a bowl, mash to a paste, then add the lemon rind. Squeeze the juice from the lemon, then, using the fork, whisk the remaining olive oil and the lemon juice into the garlic mixture. Serve the artichokes warm with the lemon dip.

COOK'S TIP

Artichokes are usually boiled, but dry-heat cooking also works very well. If you can get young artichokes, try roasting them over a barbecue.

Fava Beans with Bacon

This is a classic combination; however, for a change, or if you'd like to serve this dish to vegetarians, you can omit the chopped bacon and substitute the same quantity of drained sun-dried tomatoes in oil – it will be equally delicious.

INGREDIENTS

Serves 4

2 tablespoons olive oil
1 small onion, finely chopped
1 garlic clove, finely chopped
2 ounces rindless smoked lean bacon,
   coarsely chopped
8 ounces fava beans, thawed
   if frozen
1 teaspoon paprika
1 tablespoon sweet sherry
salt and freshly ground black pepper

1 Heat the oil in a saucepan and fry the onion, garlic and bacon over high heat for 5 minutes until softened and browned.

2 Add the beans and paprika and stir-fry for 1 minute. Add the sherry, cover, and cook for 5–10 minutes until the beans are tender. Add salt and pepper to taste.

—— COOK'S TIP ——

If you have time, remove the dull skins from the fava beans to reveal the bright green beans beneath.

Garlic Mushrooms

Provide crusty bread to mop up the creamy cooking liquid.

INGREDIENTS

Serves 4

2 tablespoons butter
8 ounces large, flat mushrooms, sliced
4 garlic cloves, thinly sliced
2 tablespoons chopped fresh parsley
2 tablespoons heavy cream
salt and freshly ground black pepper

1 Heat the butter in a large frying pan. Add the mushrooms and garlic and cook for 5 minutes until the mushrooms are tender and have released their juices.

2 Stir in the parsley and cream, season to taste and cook for 1–2 minutes more until piping hot.

—— COOK'S TIP ——

For added variety, flavor and texture, use a mixture of mushrooms, such as chestnut mushrooms, oyster mushrooms and tiny button mushrooms.

Mushrooms Stuffed with Walnuts and Tomatoes

INGREDIENTS

Serves 4

½ cup walnuts, coarsely chopped
4 sun-dried tomatoes in
  oil, drained
½ cup cream cheese
12 closed cup mushrooms, about
  8 ounces, stalks removed
1 tablespoon butter
½ cup grated Manchego or
  Cheddar cheese
salt and coarsely ground black pepper
Italian parsley, to garnish

COOK'S TIP

For a delicious variation, use only half the
filling, coat the mushrooms in flour, egg
and bread crumbs and deep-fry until crisp.

1 Place the chopped walnuts in a
small frying pan. Shake the pan
over gentle heat for 3–5 minutes until
the walnuts are golden brown. Chop
the sun-dried tomatoes.

2 Turn the walnuts into a bowl and
stir in the sun-dried tomatoes and
cream cheese, with salt and pepper to
taste. Fill the mushroom caps with
the mixture.

3 Preheat the broiler to medium.
Melt the butter in a casserole large
enough to hold all the mushrooms in a
single layer. Add the mushrooms,
stuffing-side up. Broil gently for about
7 minutes.

4 Sprinkle the mushrooms with the
cheese, and then broil for about
5 minutes more, until the cheese is
bubbling and the mushrooms are
tender. Serve hot, garnished with
Italian parsley.

Russian Salad

This colorful cold salad is a tapas bar staple.

INGREDIENTS

Serves 4

8 new potatoes, scrubbed
  and quartered
1 large carrot, diced
4 ounces fine green beans, cut into
  ³/₄-inch lengths
³/₄ cup peas
½ Spanish onion, chopped
4 cornichons or small gherkins, sliced
1 small red bell pepper, seeded and
  diced
⅓ cup pitted black olives
1 tablespoon capers
4–6 tablespoons aïoli or mayonnaise
1 tablespoon freshly squeezed
  lemon juice
2 tablespoons chopped fresh dill
freshly ground black pepper
fresh dill, to garnish

—— COOK'S TIP ——

For a sweeter flavor, roast and skin the bell
pepper before adding it to the salad.

1 Cook the potatoes and diced carrot in a saucepan of boiling, lightly salted water for 5–8 minutes until almost tender. Add the beans and peas to the pan and cook for 2 minutes more, or until all the vegetables are tender. Drain well.

2 Turn the cooked vegetables into a large bowl. Add the onion, cornichons, red bell pepper, olives and capers. Stir the aïoli or mayonnaise and lemon juice together.

3 Add most of the dressing and the dill to the vegetables with plenty of freshly ground black pepper. Toss well to coat the vegetables lightly. Chill until ready to serve, then drizzle with the remaining dressing and garnish with the dill.

Stewed Eggplant

INGREDIENTS

Serves 4

4–6 tablespoons olive oil
1 large eggplant, sliced into
 ½-inch rounds
2 shallots, thinly sliced
4 tomatoes, quartered
2 garlic cloves, thinly sliced
4 tablespoons red wine
2 tablespoons chopped fresh parsley,
 plus extra to garnish
salt and freshly ground black pepper

COOK'S TIP

For a tasty variation, spoon the cooked
mixture into a casserole, sprinkle with
grated cheese and broil for 5 minutes, until
bubbling and golden.

1 Heat 1 tablespoon of the oil in a
large frying pan. Cook the
eggplant slices in batches (adding more
oil as necessary, but reserving
1 tablespoon), until golden brown.
Drain the slices, cut them into strips
about ½ inch wide, and set aside.

2 Heat the reserved tablespoon of oil
in a saucepan and cook the shallots
for 5 minutes until golden. Add the
eggplant strips with the tomatoes, garlic
and wine. Season to taste. Cover and
simmer for 30 minutes. Stir in the
parsley, check the seasoning and serve,
sprinkled with chopped parsley.

Zucchini Fritters

Serve these crisp fritters with a
dipping sauce such as aïoli,
tomato sauce, Sherry Salsa or
Fiery Salsa.

INGREDIENTS

Serves 4

2 zucchini
¼ cup seasoned flour
2 eggs, beaten
2 tablespoons milk
vegetable oil, for frying
coarse sea salt

1 Cut the zucchini on the diagonal
into slices about ¼ inch thick. Toss
the slices in the seasoned flour in a
strong plastic bag. Beat together the
egg and milk. Heat ½ inch oil in a
frying pan.

2 Shake off the excess flour from the
zucchini slices and then dip them,
one at a time, into the egg mixture
until well coated.

3 Shallow fry the fritters in the hot
oil for 1–2 minutes on each side
until crisp and golden. Drain on paper
towels and serve, lightly sprinkled
with sea salt.

Broiled Asparagus with Salt-cured Ham

Serve this tapas when asparagus is plentiful and not too expensive.

INGREDIENTS

Serves 4
6 slices of serrano ham
12 asparagus spears
1 tablespoon olive oil
sea salt and coarsely ground black
  pepper

COOK'S TIP

If you can't find serrano ham, use Italian prosciutto or Portuguese *presunto*.

1 Preheat the broiler to high. Halve each slice of ham lengthwise and wrap one half around each of the asparagus spears.

2 Brush the ham and asparagus lightly with oil and sprinkle with salt and pepper. Place on the broiler tray. Broil for 5–6 minutes, turning frequently, until the asparagus is tender but still firm. Serve immediately.

Braised Buttery Cabbage with Chorizo

This dish is equally delicious without the chorizo sausage, so just omit it when serving this to vegetarian guests.

INGREDIENTS

Serves 4
¼ cup butter
1 teaspoon caraway seeds
8 ounces green cabbage, shredded
2 garlic cloves, finely chopped
2 ounces cured chorizo sausage,
  coarsely chopped
4 tablespoons dry sherry or white wine
salt and freshly ground black pepper

COOK'S TIP

Smoked bacon makes a good substitute for chorizo sausage in this recipe. Add it to the pan after the caraway seeds and cook for a few minutes before adding the cabbage.

1 Melt the butter in a frying pan, add the caraway seeds and cook for 1 minute. Add the cabbage to the pan with the garlic and chorizo. Stir-fry for 5 minutes until the cabbage is tender.

2 Add the sherry or wine and plenty of salt and pepper. Cover the pan and cook for 15–20 minutes until the cabbage is tender. Check the seasoning and serve.

Fried Potatoes with Aïoli

Aïoli is a Catalan specialty which began life as a mixture of garlic, salt and olive oil, pounded together with a pestle in a mortar. Nowadays, it is usually made in a food processor and is more like garlic mayonnaise.

INGREDIENTS

Serves 4
4 potatoes, peeled and cut into
   8 wedges each
vegetable oil, for deep-frying
coarse sea salt

For the aïoli
1 large egg yolk, at room temperature
1 teaspoon white wine vinegar
5 tablespoons olive oil
5 tablespoons sunflower oil
4 garlic cloves, crushed

1 Place the egg yolk and vinegar in a food processor or blender. With the motor running, add the olive oil, about 2 teaspoons at a time.

2 When all the olive oil has been added, add the sunflower oil in the same way, until the aïoli resembles a thick mayonnaise. If it is too thick, add a little more vinegar. Stir in the garlic and salt to taste. Cover and chill.

3 Heat the vegetable oil in a pan until a cube of bread turns golden in 1 minute. Add the potatoes and cook for 7 minutes until pale golden.

4 Remove the potato wedges from the pan and drain on paper towels. Raise the heat of the oil slightly – it should be hot enough to brown a cube of bread in 30 seconds. Return the potatoes to the pan and cook for 2–3 minutes until golden brown. Drain on paper towels and sprinkle with salt. Serve hot with the aïoli.

--- COOK'S TIP ---

This aïoli recipe has equal quantities of olive oil and sunflower oil, but aïoli can be made with 3 parts sunflower oil to 1 part olive oil for a milder flavor. If made solely with olive oil, the finished aïoli will have a waxy appearance and strong, slightly bitter flavor.

Spicy Potatoes

Spicy potatoes, *patatas picantes*, are among the most popular tapas dishes in Spain, where they are sometimes described as *patatas bravas* (wild potatoes). There are many variations of this classic: boiled new potatoes or large wedges of fried potato may be used, but they are perhaps best simply roasted as in this recipe.

INGREDIENTS

Serves 2–4
8 ounces small new potatoes
1 tablespoon olive oil
1 teaspoon paprika
1 teaspoon chili powder
½ teaspoon ground cumin
½ teaspoon salt
Italian parsley, to garnish

1 Preheat the oven to 400°F. Prick the skin of each potato in two or three places with a fork, then place them in a bowl.

2 Add the olive oil, paprika, chili, cumin and salt, and toss well.

3 Transfer the potatoes to a roasting pan and bake for 40 minutes.

4 Occasionally during cooking, remove the potatoes from the oven and turn them. Serve hot, garnished with Italian parsley.

— COOK'S TIP —

This dish is delicious served with tomato sauce or Fiery Salsa – provide small forks for dipping.

Artichoke Rice Cakes with Melting Manchego

For a really impressive tapas, serve these deliciously rich, cheese-filled rice cakes topped with a spoonful of aïoli and Salt-cured Salmon.

INGREDIENTS

Serves 6

1 artichoke
¼ cup butter
1 small onion, finely chopped
1 garlic clove, finely chopped
⅔ cup risotto rice
scant 2 cups hot chicken stock
¼ cup freshly grated Parmesan cheese
5 ounces Manchego cheese, very
  finely diced
3–4 tablespoons fine cornmeal
olive oil, for frying
salt and freshly ground black pepper
Italian parsley, to garnish

1 Remove the stalk, leaves and choke to leave just the heart of the artichoke; chop the heart finely.

2 Melt the butter in a saucepan and gently fry the chopped artichoke heart, onion and garlic for 5 minutes until softened. Stir in the rice and cook for about 1 minute.

3 Keeping the heat fairly high, gradually add the stock, stirring constantly until all the liquid has been absorbed and the rice is cooked – this should take about 20 minutes. Season well, then stir in the Parmesan. Transfer to a bowl. Let cool, then cover and chill for at least 2 hours.

4 Spoon about 1 tablespoon of the mixture into the palm of one hand, flatten slightly, and place a few pieces of diced cheese in the center. Shape the rice around the cheese to make a small ball. Flatten slightly, then roll in the cornmeal, shaking off any excess. Repeat with the remaining mixture to make about 12 cakes.

5 Shallow fry in hot olive oil for 4–5 minutes until the rice cakes are crisp and golden brown. Drain on paper towels and serve hot, garnished with Italian parsley.

> — COOK'S TIP —
>
> Fresh Parmesan should be piquant, grainy and not so hard that it is difficult to grate.

Classic Potato Tortilla

A traditional Spanish tortilla contains potatoes and onions. Other ingredients, such as smoked ham, chorizo or peppers, can be added, but it is generally accepted that the classic tortilla cannot be improved.

INGREDIENTS

Serves 6

1 pound potatoes, peeled
1 Spanish onion
3 tablespoons vegetable oil
4 eggs
salt and freshly ground black pepper
Italian parsley, to garnish

1 Cut the potatoes into thin slices and the onion into rings.

2 Heat 2 tablespoons of the oil in an 8-inch heavy-bottomed frying pan. Add the potatoes and the onion and cook over low heat for about 10 minutes until the potatoes are just tender. Remove from the heat.

3 In a large bowl, beat together the eggs with a little salt and pepper. Stir in the sliced potatoes and onion.

4 Heat the remaining oil in the frying pan and pour in the potato mixture. Cook gently for 5–8 minutes until the mixture is almost set.

5 Place a large plate upside-down over the pan, invert the tortilla onto the plate and then slide it back into the pan. Cook for 2–3 minutes more, until the underside of the tortilla is golden brown. Cut into wedges and serve, garnished with Italian parsley.

Index